As one of the world's longest established
and best-known travel brands,
Thomas Cook are the experts in travel.

For more than 135 years our
guidebooks have unlocked the secrets
of destinations around the world,
sharing with travellers a wealth of
experience and a passion for travel.

**Rely on Thomas Cook as your
travelling companion on your next trip
and benefit from our unique heritage.**

Thomas Cook **pocket** guides

SOUTHAMPTON

Thomas
Cook

Written by Debbie Stowe

Published by Thomas Cook Publishing
A division of Thomas Cook Tour Operations Limited
Company registration no. 3772199 England
The Thomas Cook Business Park, Unit 9, Coningsby Road,
Peterborough PE3 8SB, United Kingdom
Email: books@thomascook.com, Tel: +44 (0) 1733 416477
www.thomascookpublishing.com

Produced by Cambridge Publishing Management Limited
Burr Elm Court, Main Street, Caldecote CB23 7NU
www.cambridgepm.co.uk

ISBN: 978-1-84848-493-1

First edition © 2011 Thomas Cook Publishing
Text © Thomas Cook Publishing
Cartography supplied by Redmoor Design, Tavistock, Devon
Map data © OpenStreetMap contributors CC-BY-SA, www.openstreetmap.org,
www.creativecommons.org

Series Editor: Karen Beaulah
Production/DTP: Steven Collins

Printed and bound in Spain by GraphyCems

Cover photography © Craig Roberts/Alamy

CONTENTS

SYMBOLS KEY

The following symbols are used throughout this book:

ⓐ address ☎ telephone ⓦ website address ⓔ email
🕐 opening times ⓝ public transport connections ❶ important

The following symbols are used on the maps:

𝑖	information office	O	city
✈	airport	O	large town
➕	hospital	○	small town
🛡	police station	══	motorway
🚌	bus station	──	main road
🚆	railway station		minor road
	point of interest	──	railway
❶	numbers denote featured cafés, restaurants & venues	P🚌	park & ride

PRICE CATEGORIES

The ratings below indicate average price rates for a double
room per night, including breakfast:
£ under £70 **££** £70–100 **£££** over £100
The typical cost for a three-course meal without drinks is as
follows:
£ under £14 **££** £14–22 **£££** over £22

▶ *12th-century Bargate, one of Southampton's old city gates*

INTRODUCING
Southampton

Introduction

Even the most cursory glance at British maritime history is bound to fall upon Southampton. Still one of Europe's largest commercial ports, it features in many of history's notable naval episodes, from the departure of the Pilgrim Fathers on their pivotal expedition to the New World to the doomed maiden voyage of RMS *Titanic*. Today, more happily, it's the home of Cunard, the grande dame of cruising, and a destination for the yachting set.

It's not only seafaring history in which Southampton has played a part: it was also the birthplace of the Spitfire, the classic British fighter plane. Its military endeavours incurred the wrath of the Luftwaffe, and it suffered dreadfully in the Blitz. Since then, the city has embraced its regeneration. Currently the scene of an ambitious urban development scheme, Southampton is set to be transformed into a thriving 21st-century cultural destination.

Which is not to say that Hampshire's largest city does not already enjoy a vibrant arts scene. Powered by two universities, there's an impressive complement of cutting-edge galleries to peruse, with the most distinctive – **Bargate** (see page 44), housed in an 830-year-old city gate – aptly exemplifying Southampton's innovative fusion of the historical and the contemporary.

Away from the man-made tourist attractions are swathes of more natural terrain, including **Southampton Common** (see pages 71–3) – a glorious place to escape the urban thrum. Add to this the indescribably pretty New Forest and that iconic British holiday destination the Isle of Wight, each within half an hour's journey, and you're well placed to have your fill of fresh-air-fuelled outdoor fun.

Of course, the urban thrum might be the very reason you're in Southampton in the first place. For the sizeable student body and the up-for-it Sotonians alike, dining, nightlife and entertainment all have a zing about them in this riverside metropolis. As well as several top-class arts and cultural venues to satisfy your cerebral cravings, there's the eclectic cuisine befitting a port town and plenty of lively places to socialise. Many of these lie clustered along the buzzing gastronomic hubs of Oxford Street and Bedford Place – ideal places to kick back after a day of fresh sea air.

● Southampton's Town Quay

When to go

SEASONS & CLIMATE

Its position on England's south coast gives Southampton a more clement climate than most of its fellow UK cities. Extremes of weather are rare, with winters generally mild and wet and the best chance of hot weather – though admittedly never a certainty – in July and August. The British climate is nothing if not capricious, and you may find that a chilly, washout summer is bookended by glorious warm spells in May and October. Whenever you travel, it's wise to make sure there is something in your suitcase to fend off rain or cold. As a coastal town, Southampton does inevitably get windy at times.

Though it receives a steady stream of visitors both in its capacity as a starting point for cruises abroad and as a destination in its own right, Southampton is seldom swamped by tourists. Even if you visit during peak travel times, such as school holidays or bank holiday weekends, you are unlikely to find there's no room at the inn or that the place is uncomfortably crowded.

ANNUAL EVENTS

The city has a packed events calendar, assiduously promoted by the council and tourist office. Top of the bill is September's **PSP Southampton Boat Show**, a ten-day nautical extravaganza trumpeted as the UK's leading outdoor boat show. Over a thousand vessels descend on the area, and activities cater for everyone, from serious seafarers to those who simply want to enjoy the maritime spectacle while scoffing prawns.
ⓦ www.southamptonboatshow.com

An oft-neglected aspect of Southampton is its coruscating artistic life, and nothing better encapsulates this than the **a space** (see page 50) summer project ArtVaults, in which the city's medieval vaults provide an excitingly innovative and quirky venue for contemporary art works. The project is expected to resume in 2011 after a year off. ⓦ www.artvaults.org.uk

The full programme is too extensive to enumerate here, running the gamut from Black History Month to Film Week to Ghost Walks, but details are available on the council website's events pages ⓦ www.southampton.gov.uk and the tourist office site ⓦ www.visit-southampton.co.uk

🔺 *Southampton's marina is busy all year round*

History

Inhabited as far back as the Stone Age, the area of present-day Southampton saw settlements variously established and abandoned right up until the Norman Conquest, when the medieval town became the major port of transit between the then English capital, Winchester, and Normandy. Wine came in and wool went out – and a rather less welcome import was the Black Death, which infiltrated British shores via Southampton in 1348. These weren't happy times for the town: a decade earlier it had been sacked by Europeans who used their loot to found Monaco. In order to keep out such marauding foreigners, Edward III ordered for extensive walls to be built – parts of which are still visible.

The area developed in the Middle Ages as a centre of shipbuilding, producing such illustrious vessels as Henry V's flagship HMS *Grace Dieu*. Southampton's coastal location also lent itself to military embarkation, which has continued right up until the modern era, and tourism. In the 18th century, moneyed holidaymakers came for bathing and spa sojourns. A century later, Victorian expansion saw docks and the railway come to town, earning the city the appellation 'the Gateway to the Empire'.

Boats, big both physically and symbolically, dominate the town's history, from the *Mayflower*, which carried the Pilgrim Fathers off towards the New World in 1620 (although a leak saw them abort the voyage and try 'take two' from Devon) to the ill-fated RMS *Titanic*, which hit an iceberg and sank, becoming shorthand for epic disaster. In recent years nautical departures have been more auspicious, with Southampton now synonymous with cruising. The *Spitfire*, the iconic British fighter plane, is another Sotonian triumph.

Though the town's military role saw it pummelled by the Luftwaffe in World War II, some Georgian architecture and parts of the old city walls survive to this day. In 1964 Southampton was granted city status by Royal Charter. Today its historical architecture is juxtaposed with contemporary, forward-looking development, with the presence of two universities and a steady procession of cruise liners conferring the culture and leisure that lend such appeal to this south coast destination.

◑ *The memorial to the engineers of the* Titanic *in Andrews Park*

Culture

Unsurprisingly, given where it sits, there's a strong naval flavour to Southampton's cultural life. Its major annual event is a boat show (see page 8), there are maritime and *Titanic* museums and exhibitions (with a grand **Sea City Museum** planned for spring or summer 2012 – see page 64) and cruising is big, with colossal liners often seen skulking about offshore. Even the city's largest theatre – the Mayflower, which hosts big-tent West End productions and is graced by national opera and ballet companies – is nautically named.

Other Southampton institutions include the University of Southampton and Southampton Solent University, both of which make a considerable contribution to the town's cultural life through galleries and lively arts venues. The city has latched onto arts and culture in a big way, and Guildhall Square, a large area in front of its main art gallery, is being developed as a new urban space, which is tipped to become the heart of Southampton's cultural quarter. It's already taking shape, and in time will host plays, live music, festival events and light shows.

● *The Guildhall is one of the city's main music venues*

MAKING THE MOST OF
Southampton

Shopping

There can be no doubt that Southampton's flagship, in-your-face retail destination is shopping centre **WestQuay** (not to be confused with the almost identically named West Quay Retail Park next door). Making a huge splash when it opened just over a decade ago – at the time the largest city centre shopping mall in Europe – the facility is three levels of bright and breezy British mall, with lots of natural light thanks to its glass ceilings. It's all very modern and newfangled, running on geothermal energy – although such green facts probably pass by most of the Sotonians who flock here en masse to stalk the hundred or so shops within. WestQuay's success means that smaller retail destinations such as **Bargate Shopping Centre** have been somewhat eclipsed, but the latter is worth a pop-in if you prefer inside shopping on a non-mammoth scale or a mix of specialist and alternative stores and businesses. A third shopping centre, **The Mall Marlands**, lies north of WestQuay on Civic Centre Road. High street retail can be found immediately outside WestQuay on Above Bar Street and also, perhaps not surprisingly, on the High Street.

Bohemian shoppers can bypass the malls and head towards **Bedford Place**, the city's independent retail enclave. Boutiques and other one-off outlets are punctuated by alternative cafés and restaurants, in a chain-free zone that will appeal to all who eschew the corporate. Some concerns here date back well over a century.

Market enthusiasts too are amply catered for. The area around Bargate hosts several markets, mostly over the weekend.

Friday sees proceedings go all European, with olives, cheeses, fancy fruit and veg and other indulgent comestibles lined up alongside accessories, leather goods and cosmetics. On Saturday the wares change according to the season, while on the last Sunday of the month it's all about arts and crafts. The farmers' market comes to town on a Tuesday.

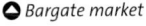

🔺 *Bargate market*

Eating & drinking

Perhaps owing to its status as a port city, Southampton is home to an array of cosmopolitan and unpretentious eateries, many of which are historical pubs of the spit-and-sawdust 'ye olde English' variety. From Italian to Indian and sushi to sandwiches, your tastes would have to be fairly exigent if you couldn't find your favoured food here. The city also seems to be generously apportioned with eye-catching eatery architecture, from traditional pubs to mini-palaces hosting Asian restaurants. Its situation on the coast means that fish fans should find their preferences satisfied.

While some restaurants and cafés serve meals in sittings, closing between lunch and dinner, others stay open for the duration of the day. Most restaurants close by 22.00, so don't come expecting continental late-night dining to be the norm, though some outlets do serve food until 23.00.

Southampton's various gastronomic hubs have markedly different vibes. Wall-to-wall restaurants stretch along and around Oxford Street, making this the city's indisputable dining hub. On weekend evenings it's lively and atmospheric, as groups throng the streets and pack the eateries and bars, lending the whole area an excited buzz. Another culinary destination, more daytime than nocturnal, is Bedford Place, the bastion of independent trade, where there's a good choice of autonomous cafés and delis. If you're after the tried-and-trusted chains, most of the big names can be found either on or around Above Bar Street or in one of the larger retail centres, such as WestQuay.

Southampton's vast tracts of green space afford ample picnicking opportunities, providing the weather is kind. Pick up some goodies from the market, if there's one on, or a sandwich shop, deli or supermarket, and either choose a pleasant spot on the grass or stake your claim on a bench.

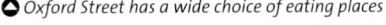

⬥ Oxford Street has a wide choice of eating places

Entertainment

A sizeable student population combined with its port city heritage give Southampton a vigorous nightlife scene, and the town's revellers exude an up-for-it vibe common to many coastal spots. A wide variety of venues compete for your custom after dark. If you're after cosy and cheerful with a tourist slant, snuggle into a booth in one of the city's historic pubs, which are all wooden beams and low ceilings. At the other end of the spectrum are unashamedly trendy, super-modern nightclubs, where things thump on well into the wee hours. The High Street is fertile pub territory but if you're after more alternative nocturnal revelry, head north to the Polygon area, where many of the students get their jollies in the bars and clubs. For all your entertainment under one roof, Leisure World on West Quay Road houses a casino, a multiplex cinema and a super-club plus a slew of restaurants and bars.

Live music is staged in diverse locations. The biggies are the **Guildhall** and **Mayflower Theatre** (see pages 68 and 69) – the latter having hosted headline acts from David Bowie to Amy Winehouse as well as the more refined strains of classical music and some drama. Several smaller venues also play host to musicians, including pubs and clubs, where you just might spot the next Craig David (incidentally, a local lad). The cultural quarter outside Guildhall is set to become the future scene of street performances and multifarious cultural goings on. Tickets for events can typically be bought from the on-site box office, as well as from tourist offices and, in the case of the larger venues, online.

The city has a fair complement of cinemas, from multiplexes showing the latest Hollywood blockbusters, like the Odeon and Cineworld, to the **Harbour Lights Picture House** (see page 59), which offers more alternative visual fare.

▲ *The Harbour Lights Picture House in Ocean Village*

Sport & relaxation

Messing about in boats is obviously an option on the sport and relaxation front, given Southampton's coastal location. Several watersports centres facilitate your getting wet and wild (and there are also three swimming pools – The Quays Swimming and Diving Complex, Bitterne Leisure Centre and Oaklands Pool – if you'd rather just get wet). If your holiday budget is really generous you could even charter a yacht. **Southampton Water Activities Centre** (ⓦ www.swac.co.uk) offers an extensive array of aquatic courses, including trips on the nearby rivers and to the Isle of Wight.

Indeed, the Isle of Wight and the New Forest are both promising ports of call for outside recreation pursuits. Each offers stunning walking trails that showcase rural England at its more glorious, and you can also cycle, ride horses, sail, plough the water in unfathomably diverse ways and disport yourself otherwise in the fresh air and impossibly scenic landscapes.

If your proclivities tend towards spectating rather than participating, take in a game of football at St Mary's Stadium, home of **Southampton FC**. In 2010 the Saints celebrated their 125th birthday, so a Saturday afternoon's footie also has a historical element. After 27 heady years of top-flight football, recent times have brought relegation, administration and sundry financial woes. Nonetheless, supporters can take heart in the equally tough times endured by bitter rivals Portsmouth. Match tickets are available online and the club also runs stadium tours ⓐ Britannia Road ⓣ 08456 889 448 ⓦ www.saintsfc.co.uk

Should roaring along with the Saints not appeal, more civilised relaxation can be indulged in at one of the city's spas, which tend to be found at the posher hotels. This is another recreation with a history: Southampton first became a spa town in 1740.

🔺 *St Mary's Stadium, home of Southampton FC*

Accommodation

Visitors to Southampton tend to be business people or cruise passengers passing a couple of days in town before or after setting sail, so there is not a profusion of low-cost lodgings tailored to the budget traveller. However, some good-value business hotels can be found in central locations, and the compact size of the city means that few beds are located far from the action. Among the modern, functional hotels that make up the bulk of the available accommodation are some wonderfully long-standing inns, some centuries old.

The leafy residential streets north of the station, en route to the common and the university, contain small enclaves of guesthouses, and fertile B&B territory can be found in the student area known as the Polygon as well as on Landguard Road, Hill Lane and Howard Road. However, you won't find the roads packed wall to wall with guesthouses as you might in more touristy south coast towns such as Brighton or Plymouth. Wandering the streets and hoping to happen upon a vacancy is therefore probably not the best option if you're luggage laden.

A more scenic option for your lodgings would be to base yourself in one of the excursion destinations – the New Forest or the Isle of Wight – rather than in the city itself; a couple of listings are included below in case you'd rather do that.

Alcantara Guest House £ Pleasantly done out and equipped with wireless internet, this family-run B&B offers on-site parking and a mix of en-suite and non-en-suite rooms. Rates

include a full English breakfast with a vegetarian option. Check the website for special offers for longer stays. ⓐ 20 Howard Road ⓣ 023 8033 2966 ⓦ www.alcantaraguesthouse.co.uk

Asturias House £ Asturias House provides self-catering accommodation that aims to be a cost-efficient alternative to a 4-star hotel for short or long stays. Kitchens are shared and come with laundry facilities. ⓐ 22 Howard Road ⓣ 023 8022 3372 ⓦ www.asturiashouse.co.uk

Banister Guest House £ Flat-screen televisions and free Wi-Fi are among the amenities at this family concern, which offers good-value, unfussy accommodation. There's a lounge and a dining room where guests can consume takeaway food. ⓐ 11 Brighton Road ⓣ 023 8022 1279 ⓦ www.banisterhouse.co.uk

Ibis £ In the same complex as the Novotel, the reliable 2-star Ibis offers clean, comfortable budget accommodation. Rooms come with cable TV and tea- and coffee-making facilities. Both the train station and the ferry port are only minutes away. ⓐ West Quay Road, Western Esplanade ⓣ 023 8063 4463 ⓦ www.ibishotel.com

The Winston Hotel £ Simple budget lodgings not far from Southampton Common, with a choice of en-suite or shared bathroom facilities. This traditional establishment extends a warm welcome to all comers. Downstairs is a large pub with some outside seating and a bar menu. ⓐ 51 Archers Road ⓣ 023 8022 4404 ⓦ www.thewinstonhotel.co.uk

Jurys Inn ££ Located next to the swathe of parkland that dominates the centre of town, this branch of the ever-dependable Jurys Inn chain provides welcoming service and more than adequate facilities. Smartly decorated rooms are larger than the norm for such a central location, and very comfortable too. There's a restaurant, bar and coffee bar on-site. ⓐ Charlotte Place ⓣ 023 8037 1111 ⓦ http://southamptonhotels.jurysinns.com

The Star Hotel ££ If you want pedigree and convenience, this four-century-old former coaching inn is the place – past royals, no less, have lain down their weary heads on its pillows. Rooms retain a certain English tweeness about the décor, but all come with colour televisions and complimentary tea and coffee. Take your meals in the restaurant. ⓐ 26 High Street ⓣ 023 8033 9939 ⓦ www.starhotel.co.uk

Dolphin Hotel ££–£££ Extensive renovation has seen this historical hostelry emerge as a luxury 4-star property radiating class, style and confidence. You can eat and drink in the hotel in similarly elegant surroundings; several succulent-sounding meat mains vie to please your palate in Signature Restaurant. ⓐ 34–35 High Street ⓣ 023 8038 6460 ⓦ www.dolphin-southampton.com

Novotel ££–£££ Just minutes from the station, the 3-star Novotel is located in a quiet hotel complex, a short walk from the centre of town. Your entrance is heralded by a futuristic lobby, complete with Big Brother diary-room-style chairs. Rooms are done out in contemporary style, beds are wonderfully comfortable and there's a pool and gym. ⓐ 1 West Quay Road, Western Esplanade ⓣ 023 8033 0550 ⓦ www.novotel.com

White Star Tavern £££ Swanky boutique accommodation that boasts touches of finery such as Egyptian cotton sheets adorning king-size beds, indulgently big showers and an award-winning restaurant in the building. Southampton digs don't get much more upscale than the White Star, which takes its name from the renowned shipping firm. ⓐ 28 Oxford Street ⓣ 023 8082 1990 ⓦ www.whitestartavern.co.uk

ISLE OF WIGHT
Yelfs Hotel £ The recently refurbished rooms at Yelfs, one of Ryde's town's oldest hotels, have undergone a smart sprucing up and can sleep up to four people. Some enjoy Solent views. Self-catering accommodation is available in Bromley House, a new addition to the property. ⓐ 54 Union Street, Ryde ⓣ 01983 564062 ⓦ www.yelfshotel.com

THE NEW FOREST
New Forest Hotels £££ This small group of properties comprises four distinctive New Forest country house hotels, in Cadnam, Beaulieu, Lyndhurst and Burley, respectively. Sumptuous rooms exude quality, and some have luxurious touches such as four-poster beds and fluffy dressing gowns. ⓣ 0800 444 441 ⓦ www.newforesthotels.co.uk

THE BEST OF SOUTHAMPTON

Whether it's the city's nautical pedigree, forward-looking arts scene, copious green space or the two classic excursions on its doorstep, Southampton is bound to offer something that floats your boat.

TOP 10 ATTRACTIONS

- **Park life** It's billed as the greenest city in southern England, and Southampton's surfeit of green spaces is verdant proof that the tag is merited (see pages 61–3).

- **Galleries** Innovative art installations are a go-go, everywhere from the city's subterranean vaults and medieval walls to the University of Southampton campus (see pages 49 and 73).

- **Bargate** Slap bang in the middle of the modern main street, the eye-catching Grade-I-listed Norman gate has housed a guildhall, a prison and an art gallery (see page 44).

- **Old Town** The quirky names of its fortifications – God's House and Catchcold Tower – give a flavour of Southampton's little-known Old Town, where historical delights await around the most unpromising of corners (see page 48).

- **Mayflower Theatre** Enjoy a slice of London's West End at the Grade-II-listed theatre, the largest in the south of England, where one big-name musical follows hard on the heels of another (see page 69).

- **Maritime traditions** Big boats are what Southampton is all about and its backdrop of gargantuan cruise liners is a spectacular reminder of the city's maritime traditions (see pages 46–7).

- **Isle of Wight** England's largest island has been pulling in the tourists since Victorian times, and its bucolic charms will not disappoint (see pages 78–82).

- **The New Forest** Dappled hollows and rolling fields as far as the eye can see – this is England's green and pleasant land writ large (see pages 83–8).

- **Solent Sky Aviation Museum** Walk among the UK's illustrious aircraft history at this museum, home to the iconic *Spitfire*, the emblem of British pluck and derring-do (see page 52).

- **St Mary's Stadium** You'll want to be in that number when the Saints go marching in the stadium which houses Southampton's embattled football team (see page 20).

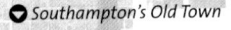 *Southampton's Old Town*

Suggested itineraries

HALF-DAY: SOUTHAMPTON IN A HURRY

Assuming you have the weather for it, a brief walk from north to south will show you the best of the city. Start at **Guildhall Square**, which in its new function as the heart of the cultural quarter, may be hosting some activity; in any case, you're right by the **City Art Gallery**, which is small enough to scoot around in 15–20 minutes. On exiting the building, proceed forwards into East Park and wend your way south to take in Southampton's beautiful urban greenery and its various memorials. At the end of the park, head right towards **Bargate** (see page 44), the remarkable structure that bridges the city's main thoroughfare. Go left and continue down the High Street, stopping to view the **Holyrood Church** ruins (see pages 44–6) on your left, **St Michael's Church** (see page 49) and the clutch of historical buildings on your right, including the city walls. Bear left and round things off with lunch or dinner on Oxford Street.

1 DAY: TIME TO SEE A LITTLE MORE

Sticking to the same basic route as above, your schedule now allows for more time at each attraction. You can also stop and have a nose around some of the city's museums. Several are clustered in the Old Town, at the bottom end of the High Street; pick according to your predilections. Plane enthusiasts will enjoy the **Solent Sky Aviation Museum** (see pages 52–3) beyond Oxford Street. If your day extends into a night, see what's on at the **Mayflower Theatre** (see page 69) or take in some live music in a historical pub.

2–3 DAYS: SHORT CITY-BREAK

Your next priority should be to go north, mainly to enjoy the common, but also to see the university, whether for its **John Hansard Gallery** (see page 73) or for an evening event at its concert hall or theatre. For downtime, make for the exquisite New Forest.

LONGER: ENJOYING SOUTHAMPTON TO THE FULL

As well as ticking off both the New Forest and the Isle of Wight (perhaps overnighting at one or both), you can also fully explore Southampton, incorporating the more esoteric attractions and having your fill of watersports and leisurely mooching.

◗ *East Park's trees in autumn splendour*

Something for nothing

Southampton is an obliging host for the free-seeking and frugal, with many of its highlights either outside and entirely accessible, or inside but still gratis. Of course, the parks and common cost nothing to visit; don't worry about an unexpected downpour catching you out on the common, as the **Hawthorns Urban Wildlife Centre** (see pages 70–71) has a free (indoor) exhibition and bargain café which permits the consumption of packed lunches. **The Holyrood Church ruins** (see pages 44–6), replete with their two audio stations (one of which features moving stories about the *Titanic*), offer an absorbing and moving historical insight with no charge. Art lovers can indulge their passion without paying a penny – the **John Hansard Gallery** and **City Art Gallery** (see pages 73 and 64) have free entry; the former even promises a complimentary tea or coffee. Turner Sims at the university stages frequent free lunchtime concerts.

Exploring the **Old Town** (see page 48) – the city walls, **St Michael's Church** (see page 49), **Tudor House Museum**, if it has reopened (see page 54) – will not trouble your wallet, and free guided heritage walks are also organised. While some of the attractions in that area do charge entry fees, many of their buildings are impressive enough that even their exteriors merit examination. The local scenery – from the city itself to the New Forest – is well worth your time. In town, that includes admiring the cruise liners that ply their way into and out of the port; a sheet with the weekly cruise timings is available from the tourist office. Sadly the cruises themselves do not fit into the freebie category!

When it rains

If rain prevents enjoyment of Southampton's glorious grassland, the city boasts several indoor options. None of the museums is really big enough to absorb an entire morning or afternoon (unless your interest in the topic borders on the obsessive), so one option is to head for the Old Town, where the sights are clustered close enough together for you to dash between them during any breaks in the downpour. Daytime performances – such as the occasional matinee at the Mayflower or Nuffield or a lunchtime concert at Turner Sims – can help pass the time in an agreeable fashion if the rain appears to have set in for the duration. Should you be in the City Art Gallery when wet weather strikes, the central library in the same building affords opportunities for general browsing as well as delving into the local history. In the same area, the archives include a collection of oral history interviews (🅰 Ground floor of the south block of the Civic Centre 🕐 10.00–16.00 Tues, Wed & Thur).

Inclement weather also provides an excuse to indulge in a spot of mall shopping – enormous WestQuay being the obvious first choice – or to hole up in one of the entertainment complexes that you might ordinarily discount for being too frivolous for your holiday time – try Ocean Village if you're in the southeast of town or West Quay Retail Park to the west. Cinemas, shops, restaurants and bars await. Ocean Village also offers marina views, so you can get in a poetic mood watching the rains lash the river. The wall-to-wall bistros and cafés on Oxford Street and, to a lesser extent, Bedford Place can also provide welcome shelter-plus-victuals from the elements.

On arrival

ARRIVING
By air

Southampton's airport is in Eastleigh, on the outskirts of the city
(ⓦ www.southamptonairport.com). It's not large, but has the
staples you are likely to need: car rental outlets (in a separate
building across the road from the terminal) and Mitchell's Bar &
Kitchen if you're peckish. Trains and buses both serve the city
centre. Come out of the main exit and go left to reach the
railway station, Southampton Airport Parkway, from where direct
trains to Southampton Central depart every ten minutes (less
frequently late at night), starting just after 06.00 and running
through to about 01.30, with a journey time of between seven
and eleven minutes (ⓦ www.nationalrail.co.uk). The fare is cheap
and cannot be beaten on price or convenience if you're going to
the city centre, though an alternative is to take the bus. The Uni-
link U1C serves the University of Southampton, city centre and
Eastern Docks (ⓦ www.unilinkbus.co.uk). Departures from
outside the main airport exit are every 10 minutes on weekdays
(every 20 minutes in the evenings). Services run from about
05.30 to just before 23.30. The main concourse has a taxi desk for
booking cabs into town around the clock. Taxis also wait at the
airport, but a pre-booked vehicle will charge about two-thirds of
the price.

By car

The M3, M27 and A34 are the main roads you'll take if you're
coming from London or more generally from the north (which is

likely – if you're coming from the south, you're probably on a boat). From the M3, the A33 brings you directly into the heart of town. Parking is not too problematic by British city standards; there are several car parks in the centre which are well signed on the whole. You'll find some spots where parking is free for two hours, and out of the centre leaving your car on the street may be free altogether. Meticulous types can find a wealth of parking information on the council website, including the location and costs of parking, or pick up a copy of the leaflet with the same details. The Southampton Romanse site (ⓦ http://southampton.romanse.org.uk) also provides traffic and travel information.

By coach

Close to the railway station and even more central is the city's coach terminus, on Harbour Parade. If you pitch up here, it's just a few minutes' walk to WestQuay, Bargate or the Civic Centre. The place is not overburdened with facilities, but you're so close to town that it's unlikely to matter.

By rail

Trains chug into Southampton Central Station, which is as conveniently located as its name suggests, not far from the Mayflower Theatre to the northwest of the main drag. From here it's possible to reach the action on foot, though as the station is nestled among the city's retail parks it's not the most aesthetically scintillating of walks. In any case, a free bus service shuttles between the station (come out on the side of platform 4 and turn left), West Quay and Town Quay for the Isle of Wight

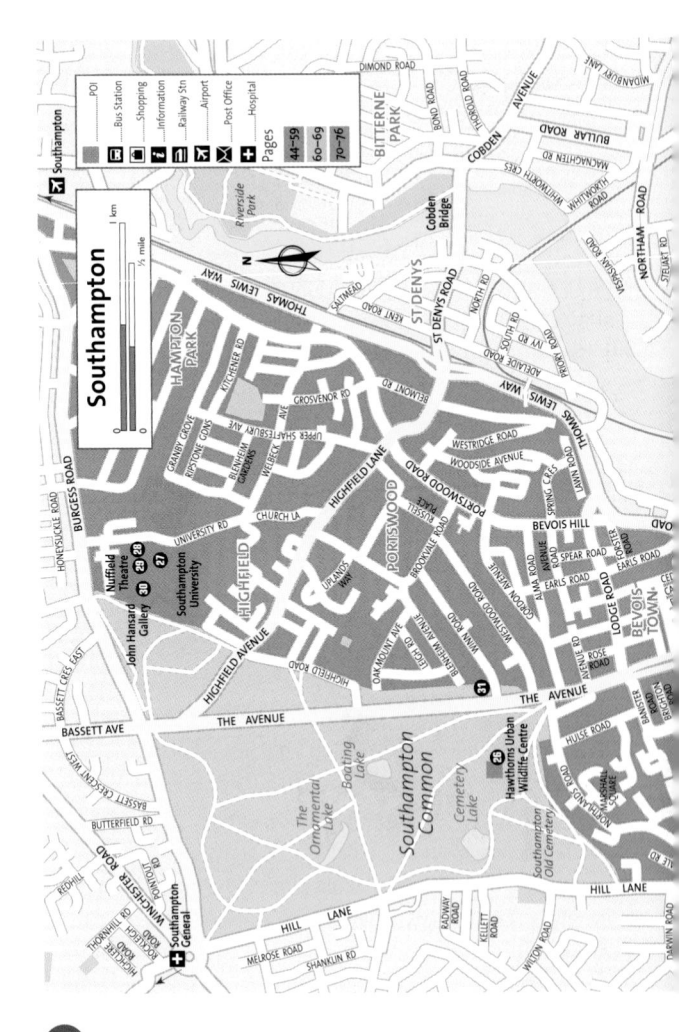

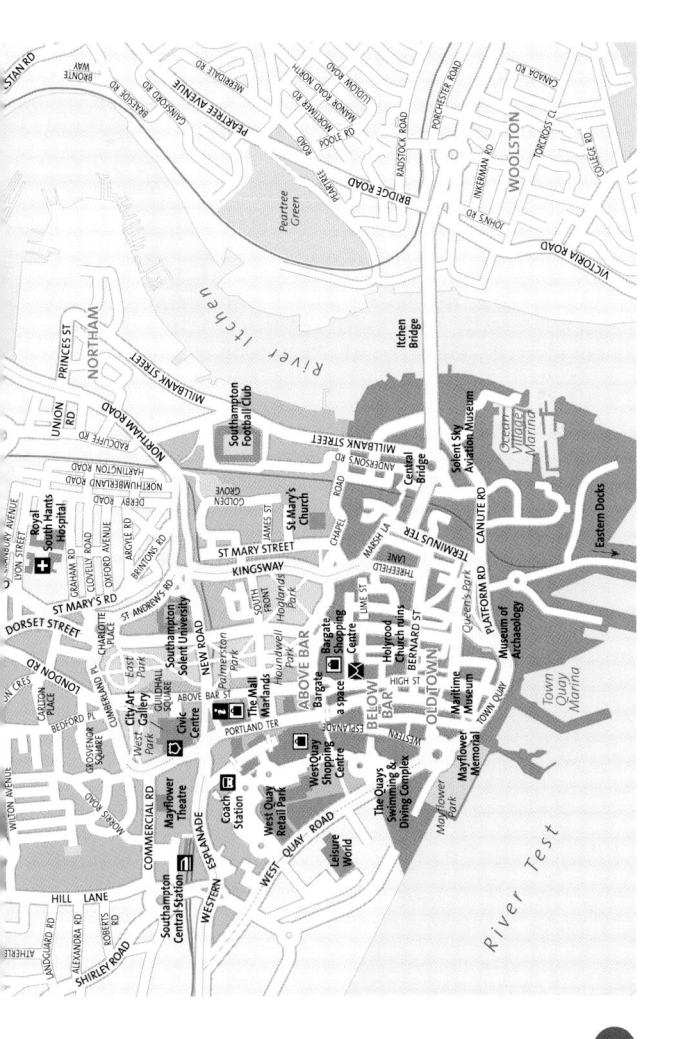

ferry, up to every quarter of an hour, between 07.00 or 08.30 and 20.30 or 20.45, depending on the day. This generally obviates the need for a taxi within the above times, but there is a rank should you require one.

FINDING YOUR FEET

Not being huge, and having natural river borders – the Itchen and the Test – Southampton is a fairly easy place to get around, even for those whose sense of navigation is not their strong point. The city centre's main artery is the north–south thoroughfare that turns from The Avenue into London Road, then Above Bar Street and finally High Street as it gets further south. Use this street to get your bearings. The Civic Centre clock tower ('Kimber's Chimney' to locals) is another useful orientation point. So too, theoretically, are the names of the districts immediately to the north and south of Bargate – Above Bar and Below Bar respectively. However, some long-term Sotonians are not familiar with the designations, so they might be of limited assistance. A couple of doppelgänger names may confuse the first-time visitor. Town Quay refers to both the quay itself and the road it is on; here, for clarity, the latter is called Town Quay Road. And WestQuay is distinct from West Quay Retail Park – although they are next to each other.

GETTING AROUND

The heart of the city, taken to include the Civic Centre, Above Bar and Below Bar, Old Town, Oxford Street and the docks, is reasonably compact and much of it is pedestrianised. The common and the University of Southampton, however, are at

⬥ *Southampton is the cruise capital of northern Europe*

some remove, and if you decide to walk, you're in for something of a trek. Accordingly, the city's bus network can come in handy – as it can too for getting between points in the centre if you're pushed for time or suffering from sightseeing fatigue. Public transport within the town means buses, which are run by different companies (see page 91). The council website (Ⓦ www.southampton.gov.uk) hosts a useful public transport map, along with frequency of services and where to catch your bus.

Your own wheels, while not necessary for much of the centre, may be useful for visiting the common or the University of Southampton and will definitely come into their own for excursions out of the city. If you're only going to make the odd vehicular foray, taxis may suffice. Hackney carriages, which in Southampton are predominantly white and have a roof sign confirming their status, can be hailed. You can also queue in taxi ranks at expected spots around town. Private cabs must be booked by phone and tend to be cheaper than their hackney counterparts. Another way to secure your independence from the vicissitudes of public transport is to hop on your bike. The city has some cycle lanes, though by no means a comprehensive network. The council provides a cycling map on its website and also produces an accompanying bike guide.

Visitors to the New Forest from Southampton have several public transport options. Frequent trains go from Southampton Central to Brockenhurst, taking around 15–20 minutes and costing just over £5 (Ⓦ www.nationalrail.co.uk). Other stations in the national park are Ashurst, Beaulieu Road and the charmingly named Sway, while Hinton Admiral, Lymington, New Milton and

Totton are all nearby. Buses also go between Southampton and the New Forest, though it's wise to do your research before setting off, as some services only run hourly. In season, take the New Forest Tour, an open-top bus service that allows passengers to hop on and off (Ⓦ www.thenewforesttour.info). The bus can also take bikes, so is a handy way to combine covering tracts of the park with some cycling. Another more scenic option is the Hythe Ferry, which runs throughout the year from the Town Quay (Ⓦ www.hytheferry.co.uk).

If you fancy popping over to the Isle of Wight, it's a case of taking to the high seas. Prepare to dig deep for the privilege – the passage there is said to be the most expensive ferry journey

🔺 The ferry that runs between Southampton and Hythe

per mile in the world. Red Funnel (ⓦ www.redfunnel.co.uk), the old-timer on the scene, operates an hourly (every hour and a half in winter) passenger-vehicle ferry service to East Cowes, which takes just under an hour. To (West) Cowes it runs a more frequent high-speed catamaran, carrying foot passengers only, with a journey time of 25 minutes. Private operators also run tours over to the island. If you're combining the Isle of Wight and the New Forest on a mini-tour, Wightlink (ⓦ www.wightlink.co.uk) runs a 30-minute car ferry service between Lymington and Yarmouth, which keeps to a fairly frequent timetable even in winter. Booking ahead online may help keep the cost down. Sadly, unless you decide to go from nearby Portsmouth or Southsea, you won't be able to make the oft-repeated Beatles joke of asking for 'a ticket to Ryde'.

Car hire
Should you wish to rent a car for your stay – which could be useful for out-of-town excursions and even for nipping up to the common and the University of Southampton – the city has several rental outlets (see page 91). If you're flying in, simply head straight to the designated car-hire building opposite the airport terminal.

◉ *A surviving tower in the old city walls*

THE CITY OF
Southampton

Introduction to city areas

The city has been split into three areas, moving from south to north. The first two directly adjoin each other, with Bargate marking their border. The third area covers the University of Southampton and Common, at a slight distance from the heart of town.

South of Bargate includes the Old Town – often neglected by natives of the city – many of the museums and Ocean Village. Town Quay, from where ferries sally forth to the Isle of Wight, can also be found here, and from this part of the city it is possible to view the huge cruise liners as they sail in and out.

Around the Civic Centre is Southampton's modern heart, exemplified by Guildhall Square, set to be the hub of the new cultural quarter. The area is home to a gallery, two arts venues, the local BBC headquarters and the gigantic WestQuay, not to mention numerous other retail outlets. It's also bisected by a chain of parks, and Southampton Solent University campus lies next to these parks.

North of the centre, Southampton Common and the University of Southampton are both well worth the detour.

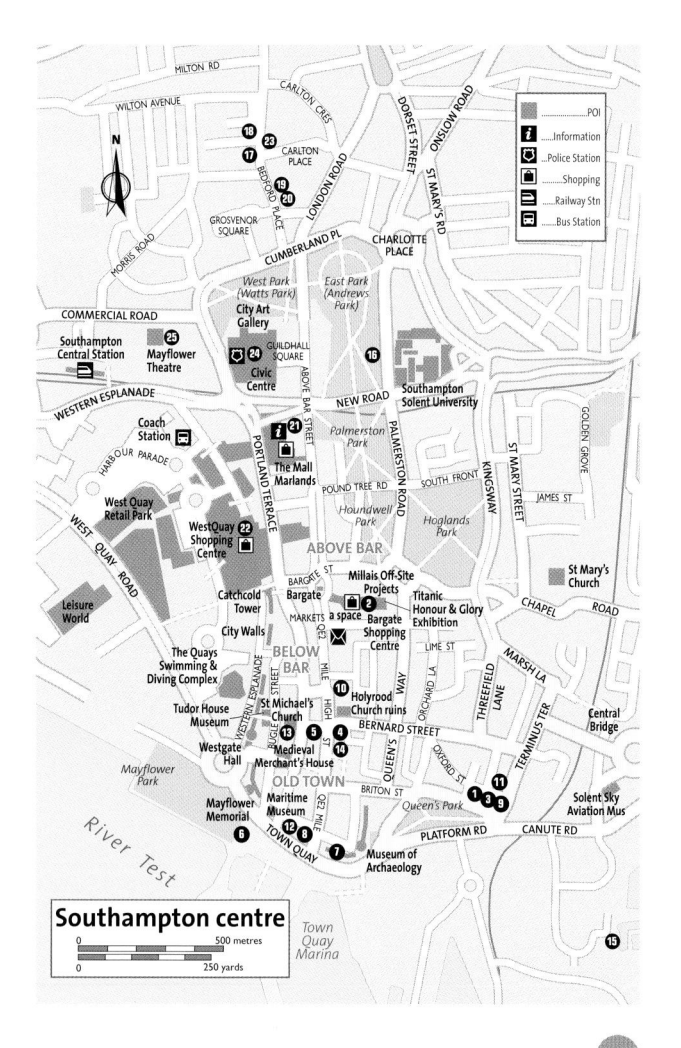

Southampton centre

Town Quay Marina

South of Bargate

The tourist heart of Southampton is the district below Bargate, which stretches from the monument itself right down to the riverside. It encompasses not only the city's Old Town and many of its museums but also the much more contemporary Ocean Village Marina. This part of town is the place for boat-spotting, whether it's yachts or cruise ships you're keen to scout. The area is mostly walkable, though the zone around Ocean Village is at a slight remove – it is, however, served by the U1 and U6 buses.

SIGHTS & ATTRACTIONS

Bargate

Sitting in the middle of Southampton's modern main street is this large gate, the best preserved of a total of seven. Since being erected in Norman times as part of the city's fortifications, the Grade I-listed building, once the entrance to the Old Town, has served as a prison and a police station. The construction is much more intricate than you might expect from a mere gate. Over the centuries it has been enhanced with lions, monarchs, a bell and a sundial. Today it makes an arresting oasis of history in a desert of modernity, and houses an art gallery, **a space** (see page 50).

ⓐ On junction of Above Bar Street and High Street

Holyrood Church ruins

Inconspicuously set back off the High Street, the ruins of this old church stand as a poignant memorial both to naval personnel who perished at sea and to the victims of a parish fire in 1837.

One of the five original churches serving the old walled town, Holyrood was built in 1320 and suffered damage during the Blitz in 1940. Prior to that, it was patronised by the Crusaders departing for the Holy Land, 15th-century soldiers en route to Agincourt and Philip II of Spain in advance of his Winchester

RMS *TITANIC*

The largest passenger steamship in the world. The most advanced technologies of the time. Unsinkable. In the century since the famously unsinkable ship sank, the *Titanic* has become synonymous with grand-scale, hubristic disaster. Four days after setting off on her maiden voyage from Southampton to New York, she hit an iceberg, and two hours and 40 minutes later took down 1,517 of the 2,227 people on board to a watery grave. Though safety law had been observed, the too few lifeboats departed the stricken vessel half-empty, as crew members who had misunderstood the 'women and children first' protocol prevented men from boarding them. The massive loss of life (almost unprecedented in peacetime), the enormity of the ship, tragically ironic assurances of its unsinkability and many legends associated with the catastrophe have seared the story into the public imagination. It has since spawned numerous films, including James Cameron's 1997 blockbuster, whose gargantuan costs and Oscar haul seemed somehow to pay tribute to the ambition of the initial project itself.

Cathedral marriage to Queen Mary. As well as the shell of the church, there is a separate *Titanic* memorial. Two audio stations provide descriptive information on how the church has looked over time and moving testimonies on the sinking of the *Titanic*, including the heart-rending story of a woman whose father went down with the ship. Though it is just off the busy High Street, the memorial exudes a solemn serenity, and is a peaceful place to contemplate the fates of those in peril on the sea. The chancel is now sometimes used for temporary exhibitions and musical performances. ⓐ Corner of High Street and Bernard Street ⓣ 023 8063 5904 ⓘ 24 hours

Mayflower Memorial

Erected nearly a century ago, this monument commemorates the departure of the Pilgrim Fathers as they quit what they perceived as their licentious and oppressive homeland and made for the New World. A copper replica of the vessel joins various plaques in honour of both the Pilgrims themselves and the US troops who set off from Southampton in their footsteps more than three centuries later. ⓐ Opposite Mayflower Park ⓘ 023 8083 3333

Mayflower Park

Pretty Mayflower Park distinguishes itself from Southampton's abundance of attractive green space by its vantage point: from here you can watch cruise liners as they wend their grand way into or out of town (would-be ship spotters can pick up a weekly schedule from the tourist office). Aside from the official cruise ship viewing point – essentially some sheltered benches in the southwest corner – there's also a children's playground and snack vendor. ⓐ South of junction of West Quay Road and Town Quay Road, between Dock Gates 7 and 8 ⓘ 023 8083 3605 ⓛ Approximately daylight hours

Medieval Merchant's House

Already a beneficiary of the expensive renovation programme sweeping some of Southampton's historical sights, this 13th-century house now contains many period features and is alleged to be haunted. A Grade-I-listed building, it was built by

▲ *The 13th-century Merchant's House*

John Fortin, the merchant who lived and did business on the premises. Sensitive restoration has expunged the property of some of its more recent additions, and today it is an atmospheric tribute to a bygone age, its creaky beams oozing medieval spirit. ⓐ 58 French Street ⓣ 023 8022 1503 ⓦ www.english-heritage.org.uk ⓛ Yet to be confirmed – consult website ⓘ Admission charge

Old Town

Ignored by many of the town's residents, the Old Town is a charming microcosm of ye olde England. Medieval edifices lurk around each corner along with parts of the old city walls, and while some are formal tourist attractions with entrance fees, others are historical pubs where you can sup on a traditional ale, enjoying the low-ceilinged, beamed atmosphere as you go. In contrast to the busy area to the north, the streets are sometimes almost deserted here, which only seems to add to the evocative ambience. The city walls are bedecked by plaques detailing that particular section's story or imparting a historical anecdote. Many of the museums are also in this district, so if you prefer to let serendipity dictate your schedule, wander a while here and you're bound to reach somewhere of import. ⓐ Between Below Bar and Mayflower Park

QE2 Mile

Forty cast-iron plates set in the pavement contain quotations pertaining to the city's history. A QE2 anchor, donated by shipping firm Cunard, is due to join them soon. ⓐ From Bargate to Town Quay

St Michael's Church

Southampton's oldest still-in-use building dates way back to 1070, when the Norman town was being built, and was the civic church until 1835. It was the only parish church in the centre of town to escape destruction in 1940, when the city lost seven of its places of worship. Inside it's agreeably bright and airy, with whitewashed walls, stained glass windows, an ornate, medieval, marble Belgian font and a hefty 19th-century organ. ⓐ Opposite Tudor House ☏ 023 8033 0851 🕐 11.00–16.00 Mon–Fri (Easter–Sept), closed Sat; 11.00–13.30 or 14.00 Thur, closed Mon–Wed, Fri & Sat (Oct–Easter); and for services Sun (year-round)

Walks

Guided walks are available for those eager to draw upon some insider knowledge and local pointers. Heritage and themed walks on everything from cemeteries to wildlife to Halloween take place (at times, free of charge), some organised by the **Southampton Tourist Guides Association**. ☏ 023 8057 1858 ⓦ www.stga.org.uk 🕐 Regular free walks 10.30 Sun and bank holiday Mon (Oct–May); 10.30 Mon, Wed & Sun (June); 10.30 daily (July & Sept); 10.30 & 14.30 daily (Aug)

Western Esplanade

Though parts of the old city walls are visible at numerous junctures around Southampton, the sections along Western Esplanade are particularly well preserved and impressive. The 600-year-old High Arcades have been put to use in art projects such as Halation, under which they were illuminated by colour-changing linear LED strips.

Westgate Hall

Formerly known as Tudor Merchant's Hall, this erstwhile fish market reopened at the end of 2010 following a year-long refurbishment. This Grade-II-listed building can be found next to Westgate, through which archway Henry V led his men to Agincourt and the Pilgrim Fathers passed on their pioneering American odyssey. ⓐ Next to Westgate ⓣ 023 8083 3007 ⓛ Private hire only

CULTURE

a space

At the vanguard of Southampton's contemporary arts scene since it moved to the upstairs floor of **Bargate** (see page 44) about five years ago, this gallery has always championed up-and-coming young artists, providing exposure opportunities for experimental work through its innovative projects. ⓐ Upstairs in Bargate, High Street ⓣ 023 8033 8778 ⓦ www.aspacearts.org.uk ⓛ 12.00–17.00 Wed–Fri, 12.00–17.00 Sat, 12.00–16.00 Sun, closed Mon & Tues

Maritime Museum

Chief draw here is probably the *Titanic* story, which elucidates the work of the crew members, their perceptions of the ship, memories of its fateful encounter with the iceberg and the subsequent reverberations of the catastrophe over the generations. Southampton's life as a port town and host city to Cunard and its royally named ships (QVs, QMs and QEs) also get a look in. The building too – the 15th-century Wool House – has a colourful history. After the wool, the place was used as a prison, and the forgivable graffiti of 18th-century French POWs is still visible on the first floor. ⓐ Wool House, Town Quay Road ⓣ 023 8022 3941 ⓦ www.southampton.gov.uk ⓛ 10.00–18.00 Mon–Fri, 11.00–18.00 Sat & Sun (summer); 10.00–16.00 Mon–Fri, 11.00–16.00 Sat & Sun (winter) ⓘ Admission charge; wheelchair access to the ground floor only

Millais Off-Site Projects (formerly Millais Gallery)

Though its permanent site at Southampton Solent University has now closed, the gallery lives on in peripatetic form. In early 2011, the initiative was renting a site in Bargate Shopping Centre, where it was continuing its work of assisting young

🔺 The Maritime Museum tells the story of the Titanic

artists and designers to gain recognition. As the move was only destined to be temporary, consult the website to check its current location before making a special journey. ☎ 023 8031 9916 Ⓦ www.solent.ac.uk ⓔ millais.gallery@solent.ac.uk

Museum of Archaeology

Though the main focus is local, the artefacts here come from as far afield – geographically and historically – as Ancient Egypt. The museum tells the story of prehistoric, Roman, Saxon and medieval Southampton. Like the Maritime Museum, it's also housed in a building with a history: God's House Tower was once the debtors' prison and felons' jail. The entrance is not immediately apparent – go through the arch and turn right. ⓐ God's House Tower, junction of High Street and Town Quay Road ☎ 023 8091 5732 Ⓦ www.southampton.gov.uk ⊙ 10.00–18.00 Thur & Fri, 11.00–18.00 Sat & Sun (summer); 10.00–16.00 Thur & Fri, 11.00–16.00 Sat & Sun (winter), closed Mon–Wed ❶ Admission charge

Solent Sky Aviation Museum

Aviation enthusiasts and children will be delighted by this museum, home to one of the most important aircraft collections in the UK. Fifteen planes are on display, some of which are the only surviving examples of their kind. The stars of the show are the Spitfire, the locally developed iconic British World War II fighter, and its designer, R J Mitchell. Solent's role as the world's most important centre for experimental and developmental work from 1908 to the late 1960s is proudly charted. ⓐ Fleet Road ☎ 023 8063 5830 Ⓦ www.spitfireonline.co.uk ⊙ 10.00–17.00

Tues–Sat, 12.00–17.00 Sun, 10.00–17.00 Mon during school holidays, last entry 16.00 ❶ Admission charge

Titanic Honour & Glory Exhibition

This interactive exhibition presents the history of British shipping, rather than just focusing on its most famous disaster. Housed in Bargate Shopping Centre (at least at the time of going to press), it is currently seeking a new waterfront home. Consult the website for its location. ⓐ Bargate Shopping Centre ⓦ www.oceanlinerexperience.co.uk 🕑 10.00–16.00 Tues–Sat, last admission 15 minutes before closing,

THE SPITFIRE

Small, effective and powered by a Rolls Royce engine and sheer British pluck, the Spitfire won the hearts of the pilots who flew it and earned a privileged place in UK military history. The single-seater fighter plane was introduced in 1938, the brainchild of Southampton-based Supermarine Aviation Works designer R J Mitchell. The only Allied fighter in production during World War II, it was used by the RAF as well as other Allies. By the end of the war, of the 27,000 Spitfires manufactured, some 8,000 had been built in Southampton. The plane continued to serve around the world until its retirement in 1961, though it will always be associated most closely with the Battle of Britain. Its performance in that decisive British victory made it a media darling, and it is fondly remembered to this day.

Closed Sun & Mon ❶ Admission charge, except for entrance to shop; cash only

Tudor House Museum

Lottery cash is currently being used extensively to overhaul this attraction, a 15th-century timber-framed house built by a local worthy. Now in the final phase of refurbishment, the site will emerge with a café extension (replete with garden views) and lift. The museum is due to reopen in summer 2011, and entry will be free. Even now it's worth ambling by simply to enjoy the impressive Tudor façade. Whether the renovation is going to have any effect on the ghosts said to the haunt the place remains to be seen. ❸ St Michael's Square ❶ 023 8033 2513 Ⓦ www.southampton.gov.uk

🔺 *Historic aeroplanes on display at the Solent Sky Aviation Museum*

RETAIL THERAPY

Bargate Shopping Centre This mall has attempted to position itself as a niche alternative to West Quay, focusing on specialist businesses rather than the usual chain names. The Internet café and Sega Park, along with PC, gaming, urban fashion and extreme sports outlets makes it popular with teenagers.
ⓐ East Bargate, just off High Street ⓣ 0870 011 0488
ⓦ www.bargatecentre.com ⓛ 09.00–19.00 Mon–Sat, 10.00–18.00 Sun & bank holidays

Ocean Village Marina Give your shopping a sprinkle of maritime glamour at this marina facility. ⓐ 2 Channel Way ⓣ 023 8022 9385 ⓦ www.mdlmarinas.co.uk

TAKING A BREAK

Southampton's foremost dining district is without doubt **Oxford Street** (ⓦ www.oxfordstreetsouthampton.co.uk) and its surrounds. This buzzy enclave comes to life after dark, especially at weekends. Another popular spot is **Ocean Village Marina** (ⓐ 2 Channel Way ⓣ 023 8022 9385 ⓦ www.mdlmarinas.co.uk), where outlets include Banana Wharf, Pitcher & Piano and Mocha Marina.

CAFÉS
The Terrace Sandwich Bar £ ❶ Unpretentious café serving hot sandwiches, jackets, toasties, salad boxes, cakes and pastries.
ⓐ 28 Queen's Terrace, right behind Queen's Park ⓣ 023 8021 2141

Shake Away ££ ❷ Bursting with youthful attitude, this bright and breezy international chain outlet pumps out funky music and lets you play table football while sampling from a bewildering smorgasbord of crazy milkshakes. ⓐ 24 Bargate Shopping Centre ☏ 023 8033 2155 ⓦ www.shakeaway.com ⏱ 10.00–17.30 Mon–Fri, 09.30–18.00 Sat, 10.30–17.00 Sun

RESTAURANTS

La Esquina £ ❸ Tapas the bona fide way, with no starters, mains or entrées, simply an array of smaller dishes, none of which break the £5 barrier. The atmosphere is cosy, laidback and leisurely, but its popularity means you sometimes have to wait a while for your food. ⓐ 40 Oxford Street ☏ 023 8022 5227 ⓦ www.laesquina tapas-restaurant.co.uk ⏱ 11.00–23.00 Mon–Thur, 11.00–24.00 Fri & Sat, closed Sun

⏶ *Ocean Village Marina is a pleasant place for dining and shopping*

Zen £–££ ❹ This funkily designed Japanese bar and restaurant has an all-you-can-eat sushi buffet (Sun–Thur 18.00–22.00) and separate (and extensive) à la carte menu. ⓐ 42 High Street, corner with Bernard Street ⓣ 023 8023 3399 ⓦ www.zen southampton.com ⓛ 12.00–15.00, 18.00–late daily

George's Restaurant ££ ❺ Dating back to 1940, this family concern is endearingly old-fashioned with photos of the owners on display and traditional hospitality guaranteed. The menu bulges with Greek and Italian comfort food. Former Prime Minister Edward Heath is among the more illustrious patrons it has welcomed over the years. ⓐ 1 St Michael's Square, opposite church ⓣ 023 8022 3749 ⓦ www.georgesrestaurant.co.uk ⓛ 11.30–14.00 daily, 17.45–22.30 Mon–Thur, 17.45–23.00 Fri & Sat, 17.45–22.00 Sun

Kuti's Royal Thai Pier ££ ❻ Looking something like Hampshire's answer to the Taj Mahal, Kuti's offers a popular buffet and a more expensive à la carte menu, and also a bar. The same company runs an Indian restaurant (ⓐ 39 Oxford Street ⓣ 023 8022 1585 ⓛ same hours as below). ⓐ The Royal Pier, Gate House, off Town Quay ⓣ 023 8033 9211 ⓦ www.kutisroyalthaipier.co.uk ⓛ 12.00–14.30, 18.00–23.30 or 24.00 daily

Platform Tavern ££ ❼ One of Southampton's pubs with a history, this quayside venue dates back to 1873. Fruit machine-free and proud, the place is done out in rich reds. Sunday roast is often accompanied by live jazz, and adjoining the pub itself is a fresh fish restaurant. ⓐ Town Quay Road ⓣ 023 8033 7232

ⓦ www.platformtavern.com **ⓛ** Food served 12.00–15.00, 18.00–21.00 Mon–Fri, 12.00–21.00 Sat & Sun

La Regata ££ **❽** Atmospheric and welcoming Spanish family venture with quay views. The à la carte menu features entrées such as fresh salmon in a cream and champagne sauce and there are also myriad tapas options including octopus. **ⓐ** Town Quay Road **ⓣ** 023 8022 3456 **ⓦ** www.laregata.co.uk **ⓛ** 12.00–14.30, 18.00–22.30 Sun–Thur, 12.00–14.30, 18.00–23.00 Fri & Sat

Scoozi ££ **❾** Italian eatery Scoozi positively buzzes when it's full, and on a weekend evening you are lucky to get a table. The young, friendly staff contributes to the fun vibe. **ⓐ** 37a Oxford Street **ⓣ** 023 8090 8700 **ⓦ** www.scoozirestaurant.com

NV ££–£££ **❿** Southampton eateries seldom come swankier-looking than this century-old Grade-II-listed former bank, while the British–European menu, which features lobster, a duck platter and venison medallions, is equally top-notch. Though some items are costly, there are some great-value set menus and offers. **ⓐ** 129 High Street **ⓣ** 023 8033 2255 **ⓦ** www.nvsouthampton.com **ⓛ** 11.30–15.00 Mon–Sat, 18.00–late Tues–Sat, 12.00–17.00 Sun

Oxford Restaurant ££–£££ **⓫** This fancy brasserie fuses British and continental cuisine into dishes such as roasted Gressingham duck breast and crisp belly of Hampshire pork. The classy interior uses a lot of dark wood and mood lighting and there are outdoor tables. **ⓐ** 35–36 Oxford Street **ⓣ** 023 8022 4444 **ⓦ** www.oxfordsrestaurant.com

Ennio's £££ ⑫ Housed in a stylishly converted Victorian warehouse, this is an acclaimed and authentic Italian trattoria. The pasta and fish are particularly recommended, and service is always convivial. ❸ Opposite ferry port ❶ 023 8022 1159 ❿ www.ennios.co.uk ❻ 12.00–14.00, 18.30–22.30 Mon–Thur, 12.00–14.00, 18.30–23.00 Fri & Sat, closed Sun

AFTER DARK

PUBS

Duke of Wellington £ ⑬ The Duke has been a public house for over five centuries, though it didn't get its current name until after the Battle of Waterloo. The place looks as you might expect, all hanging baskets and low beams. There's an aptly traditional bar menu. ❸ 36 Bugle Street ❶ 023 8033 9222 ❻ Pub 11.00–23.00 daily; food 12.00–14.30, 18.00–21.30 Mon–Sat, 12.00–14.30 Sun

Red Lion £ ⑭ Another of Southampton's historical boozers, parts of the Red Lion go way back to Norman times, though most of what you can see today is visibly Tudor. A traditional pub menu is served. ❸ 55 High Street ❶ 023 8033 3595 ❻ 11.00–23.00 Mon–Sat, 12.00–22.30 Sun

CINEMAS

Harbour Lights Picture House ⑮ A bastion of independence amid mainstream movie purveyors, Harbour Lights is part of the Picture House chain, which specialises in independent, art-house and foreign-language films. ❸ Ocean Village, 4 Ocean Way ❶ 0870 755 1237 ❿ www.picturehouses.co.uk

Around the Civic Centre

Modern Southampton pivots on the district around the Civic Centre down to Bargate, its showpiece being perhaps **WestQuay**, the massive mall that opened its doors a decade ago. The area remains the focus of the city's regeneration, with an urban cultural quarter under way up by **Guildhall** Square. But it's not all concrete and development – this section of the city also encompasses a swathe of parkland, which ensures that things never feel overwhelmingly built-up. As much of it is pedestrianised, this district is really only do-able on foot.

SIGHTS & ATTRACTIONS

Civic Centre

Heralded by the clock tower, one of Southampton's most useful landmarks, the smart Civic Centre consists of an integrated complex of buildings housing the Guildhall, council offices, public library, art gallery and police station. Though the foundation stone was laid (by the future George VI, no less) in 1930, the locale has a resolutely modern air, owing in the main to its clean, simple lines and the large, flat concreted area. This will be the much-heralded cultural quarter, centrepiece of an ambitious undertaking to provide the city with a dynamic urban space for leisure and creative pursuits. Even though it's a work in progress, the Civic Centre already hosts several arts and cultural hubs that repay a view or visit. ❸ North side of Civic Centre Road

Parks

Although technically divided into distinct parks, the city centre's green areas form one continuous verdant whole, and can therefore be treated as a unit. Starting in the northwest corner with **West Park** (sometimes known as Watts Park), the gardens curve round to the east and south to become, logically enough, **East Park** (also known as Andrews Park), then continue south into **Palmerston Park**, **Houndwell Park** and finally, off to the east, **Hoglands Park**.

The city is rightfully proud of its abundance of parks, into which much effort has been put. All possible park-related angles are covered. 'Nature in the city' information boards detail the wildlife on view. There are a few natural features, such as a pond

◠ *Southampton's Civic Centre*

◆ *The Queen's Peace Fountain in East Park*

traversed by a bridge, and some historical monuments including an affecting *Titanic* Memorial – inscription 'To the memory of the engineer officers of the RMS *Titanic* who showed their high conception of duty and their heroism by remaining at their posts, 15 April 1912'. A large Cenotaph provides equal pause for reflection. There's the pretty Queen's Peace Fountain, a 2001 embellishment, and local hymn kingpin Isaac Watts is commemorated with a statue. But the monuments are few and far enough between to preserve a sense of space. Leisure is not neglected: in addition to tennis courts for hire, and basketball, netball, 5-a-side football and volleyball facilities, a mini golf course is planned for the site of the old bowling green.
🕐 24 hours

St Mary's Church

The city's largest place of worship has origins that go back to Saxon times. The Blitz destroyed the fifth of six different churches to have stood on the site, but the Grade-II-listed sixth is now over 50 years old, with its striking spire a highlight. Aside from its aesthetic assets, St Mary's has two rather differing claims to fame. It inspired the Bing Crosby hit 'The Bells of St Mary's' (originally from 1917 and often recorded, cropping up in *Monty Python's Flying Circus* and *Goodfellas* among other places). The church football team also went on to become Southampton FC, hence their ecclesiastical nickname: the Saints. 📍 135 St Mary Street ☎ 023 8033 0851 🌐 www.sotoncitycentreparish.hampshire.org.uk 🕐 Services 09.30 Wed, 09.30 Sat, 10.30 Sun, 17.00 first and last Sun of the month

CULTURE

City Art Gallery

Its relatively small size doesn't stop Southampton's municipal art gallery packing a cultural punch. Six centuries of European art are represented, though the site's forte is 20th-century British artists such as Sutherland. A permanent collection is supplemented by two temporary exhibitions which change quarterly. The gleaming space welcomes everyone from the art cognoscenti to beginners, and there are plenty of interactive features and creative activities for children. ⓐ Civic Centre, Commercial Road ⓣ 023 8083 2277 ⓦ www.southampton. gov.uk/art ⓛ 10.00–18.00 Mon–Fri, 11.00–18.00 Sat & Sun (summer); 10.00–16.00 Mon–Fri, 11.00–16.00 Sat & Sun (winter)

New Arts Complex

Planned to open in 2012, this bold contemporary venue will bring together local company Art Asia, video and film resource City Eye, a second branch of the **Nuffield Theatre** (see page 75) and various works under the John Hansard Gallery umbrella, which together will form a dynamic new arts space. ⓐ Guildhall Square, Civic Centre ⓣ 023 8083 3498

Sea City Museum

As part of the regeneration of the Civic Centre, the old Grade-II-listed magistrates' courts will house permanent exhibitions on the *Titanic* and Southampton's role as a port city, plus temporary displays. ⓐ Old magistrates' courts, Civic Centre ⓣ 023 8083 3498

RETAIL THERAPY

Above Bar Right outside WestQuay, the Above Bar area is home to the usual retail suspects. Street performers are sometimes on hand to provide a mellifluous background to your browsing.

Bedford Place A stronghold of independent trade fighting the corporate tide, Bedford Place is home to such Southampton institutions as shoe shop WJ French & Son (ⓦ www.wjfrench andson.co.uk), a family-run concern that has been ensuring Sotonians are well shod for over two centuries. Copious other boutiques cater for the more discerning shopper.
ⓦ www.bedfordplace.co.uk

◆ *The three-storey WestQuay Shopping Centre*

City Art Gallery The creative set can take their pick of trendy diaries, postcards, stationery, jewellery and other arty accoutrements. ⓐ Civic Centre, Commercial Road ⓣ 023 8083 2277 ⓛ 10.00–18.00 Mon–Fri, 11.00–18.00 Sat & Sun (summer); 10.00–16.00 Mon–Fri, 11.00–16.00 Sat & Sun (winter)

The Mall Marlands With a mix of chain and independent retailers, the mall offers slightly smaller-scale shopping than WestQuay, with 60 shops spread over two levels. ⓐ Civic Centre Road ⓣ 023 8033 9164 ⓛ 09.00–17.30 Mon–Wed, Fri & Sat, 09.00–19.00 Thur, 10.30–17.00 Sun

WestQuay Southampton's colossal flagship retail venue is three levels of sheer, indefatigable shopping. The glass ceilings transmit copious light and there's a terrace by the food court, though it's used mainly by smokers. John Lewis and Apple are among the cornucopia of stores jostling for your pound. ⓐ Portland Terrace ⓦ www.west-quay.co.uk ⓛ 09.00–20.00 Mon–Fri, 09.00–19.00 Sat, 11.00–17.00 Sun

TAKING A BREAK

CAFÉS

ParKafe £ ⓰ As well as serving cheap-as-chips pizza, pasta and jacket potatoes, this friendly place deals with tennis, basketball, netball, 5-a-side and volleyball bookings for the park facilities. ⓐ East Park Terrace ⓣ 023 8023 0062 ⓛ 08.30–20.00 Mon–Fri, 09.30–20.00 Sat & Sun (summer); 08.30–18.00 Mon–Fri, 09.30–18.00 Sat & Sun (winter)

Room for Food £ 17 Café/deli serving up inventive sandwiches and paninis, plus sophisticated hot beverages. Customers can expect a warm welcome; takeaways available. ⓐ 81 Bedford Place ⓣ 023 8023 3523 ⓦ www.roomforfood.co.uk ⓛ 10.00–15.00 Mon–Fri, closed Sat & Sun

Yoma £ 18 Funky and friendly Yoma is refreshingly non-corporate, very much into its seasonal, local, organic and fair-trade ingredients. The café menu is imaginative and tempting, and the place occasionally hosts musical soirées. In summer you can sit outside. ⓐ 66 Bedford Place ⓣ 023 8022 2299 ⓦ www.yoma kitchen.blogspot.com ⓛ 09.00–18.00 Mon–Sat, closed Sun

RESTAURANTS

La Cucina ££ 19 Taking the sensible step of offering many of its dishes as either starter or entrée size, this trattoria does a range of salads, pizza, pasta, risotto and grills. ⓐ 10 Bedford Place ⓣ 023 8022 3388 ⓦ http://lacucinasouthampton.com ⓛ 10.00–14.30, 17.30–22.00 Mon–Thur, 10.00–14.30, 17.30–22.30 Fri & Sat, closed Sun

Fat Fig ££ 20 This small Greek taverna serves up Hellenic staples such as moussaka, king prawns and calamari. Service is Balkan style. A takeaway menu also includes decently priced paninis and wraps. ⓐ 5 Bedford Place ⓣ 023 8021 2111 ⓦ www.fatfig.co.uk ⓛ 11.00–15.00, 18.00–22.00 Mon–Fri, 11.00–23.00 Sat, closed Sun

La Tavernetta ££ 21 These genial purveyors of enjoyable Italian and Mediterranean dishes extend a warm welcome to all. The reasonably priced food is served in a relaxed atmosphere, though the bar ensures things liven up after dark. ⓐ 1–3 Civic Centre Road ⓣ 023 8063 5185 ⓦ www.latavernetta.co.uk ⓛ 11.30–22.30 daily; sometimes closing between lunch and dinner in low season

YO! Sushi ££ ㉒ The conveyor-belt sushi chain's WestQuay outlet provides a fun way to refuel mid-shop. Colour-coded dishes (indicating price) are transported round for diners to snap up at will. ⓐ Unit C2, top floor, WestQuay ⓣ 023 8008 0510 ⓦ www.yosushi.com ⓛ 12.00–20.00 Mon–Fri, 12.00–19.00 Sat, 12.00–17.00 Sun

Yuzu Lounge ££ ㉓ Asian fusion is the thing at this chic lounge bar, where trendiness emanates from the redbrick walls and high stools at the bar. Smaller portions are available, there's a tempting sharing platter and prices are way lower than the fancy environs would suggest. A DJ spins some tunes several evenings a week. ⓐ 29 Bedford Place ⓣ 023 8033 8898 ⓦ www.yuzulounge.co.uk ⓛ 12.00–late daily

AFTER DARK

ARTS VENUES
Guildhall ㉔ Graced over the years by stars of the calibre of David Bowie and Pink Floyd, and more recently by the Manic Street Preachers and Amy Winehouse, the Guildhall stages rock, pop, dance, exhibitions, comedy, fashion shows and sundry other happenings. ⓐ Civic Centre ⓣ 023 8063 2601 ⓦ www.livenation.co.uk

Mayflower Theatre ⓐ The Grade-II-listed Mayflower, which has a capacity of 2,300, stages touring West End productions, musicals, dance, opera, drama, comedy and children's shows. Tickets can be booked online, by phone, in person at the theatre box office or from the Ticket South shop at The Mall Marlands. ⓐ Commercial Road ⓣ 023 8071 1811 ⓦ www.mayflower.org.uk ⓛ Box office 09.30–20.00 Mon–Sat, 16.30–20.00 Sun (performance days); 09.30–18.00 Mon–Fri, 09.30–17.30 Sat, closed Sun (non-performance days)

⬤ *The Mayflower Theatre has 2,300 seats*

North of the centre

Some way up from the previous two parts of the city lies the final area covered by this guide. Essentially, there are two major points of interest here: Southampton Common, with its acres of bucolic charm, and the University of Southampton, whose campus is home to a cluster of cultural attractions. The two are very close together, so once you're up in this part of town it doesn't take long to get from one to the other.

Reaching this part of Southampton from the city centre is quite a hike if you're on foot. Depending on precisely where you're heading, buses 1, 2, 14, U2 and 7A are among the more useful services to save you the long walk.

SIGHTS & ATTRACTIONS

Hawthorns Urban Wildlife Centre

If you make the journey up to the common, don't miss this jolly little wildlife centre – particularly if you're with children or your interests tend towards the green. A cheerfully and thoughtfully designed information centre provides a plethora of facts on the local flora, fauna and history. Videos, touchscreens and leaflets liven things up, while children will be absorbed for eons in a dedicated room filled with microscopes, puzzles and cheery books. Not surprisingly, biodiversity and conservation are major themes, and the walls display sobering did-you-knows, such as 'There are fewer mountain gorillas in the wild than footballers in the Premier League.' Out the back is a wildlife trail that meanders around, as captions explain the various plants and features. It's all

⬤ *The Hawthorne Urban Wildlife Centre at Southampton Common*

very peaceful and pleasant, and there's a delightful terrace overlooking a pond where you can eat your own food or pick up a drink or snack from the café. Helpful staff members are around to answer any questions. The centre also organises tours of the common. ➋ Southeast corner of Southampton Common ☎ 023 8067 1921 Ⓦ www.southampton.gov.uk 🕓 10.00–17.00 Mon–Fri, 12.00–16.00 Sat & Sun (summer); 10.00–16.00 Mon–Fri, 12.00–16.00 Sat & Sun (winter)

Southampton Common

When you're standing in the middle of the 148 hectares (365 acres) of mixed wood- and grassland that make up Southampton Common, it's difficult to conceive that you are in fact still within the UK's 20th biggest city. So pastoral is the ambience that you could easily be miles from the nearest urban amenities. While its distance from the centre of town may rule out a visit if your trip is of limited duration, should you have the time, the common is a glorious place to unwind and get back to nature. Its history starts from a dispute over land rights in the 13th century, following which the borough snapped up the site and pronounced it common land; in 1844 it became a public park. Aside from the primal pleasure of being among nature, there are a few features worthy of exploration. One is **Southampton Old Cemetery** (Ⓦ www.fosoc.org) in the southwest corner. There are few burials these days, and the site serves primarily as a heritage wildlife area. Dating back to the mid-19th century, the graveyard has 45 headstones for *Titanic* victims, although the bodies were never returned to the city. There are three striking chapels, now in private hands and not open to the public. Other features include three bodies of water: the duck-frequented Cemetery Lake, Ornamental Lake – where coarse fishing is permitted with a licence – and the Boating Lake, refuge to the internationally rare great crested newt.

◑ *Get back to nature in the city on Southampton Common*

A fourth 'body of water' is the paddling pool, which is open in summer, and there are play- and keep-fit areas. Though the common is accessible round the clock, it's better to avoid going there alone at night. ⓐ Between Hill Lane and The Avenue ⓣ 023 8067 1921 ⓦ www.southampton.gov.uk ⓛ 24 hours ⓝ Bus: 1, 4, 5, U2

CULTURE

John Hansard Gallery

The bizarre sculpture on the grass outside proclaims, lest there be any doubt, that you are in the vicinity of modern art, be it in the form of painting, photography, film, installation or performance art. This university-based gallery hosts rotating exhibitions from contemporary artists, which tend to run for up to two months. Community involvement is prized here, and the gallery hosts workshops, community projects, seminars, symposia, conferences and lectures, details of which can be found on its website. Once you're on the university campus, the gallery is well signposted. ⓐ Salisbury Road ⓣ 023 8059 2158 ⓦ www.hansardgallery.org.uk ⓛ 11.00–17.00 Tues–Fri, 11.00–16.00 Sat, closed Sun, Mon, bank holidays & during exhibition installation ⓝ Bus: U1, U2, U6, 6 & 11

TAKING A BREAK

CAFÉS

Café at the Hawthorns £ ㉖ This charming little café makes an excellent spot to recharge after tiring yourself out on

Southampton Common. If the weather permits, sit outside on the serene decking area which overlooks the pond. Visitors are welcome to tuck into their own spread, but the superb-value menu – with sandwiches for £2 and cakes costing less than £1 – means there's no financial imperative to bring a packed lunch. Ice cream and hot drinks are also for sale. ⓐ Hawthorns Urban Wildlife Centre, southeast corner of Southampton Common ⓣ 023 8067 1921 ⓛ 10.30–16.30 Mon–Fri, 12.00–15.30/15.45 (eat in/take away) Sat & Sun

Refectory £–££ ㉗ Should you find yourself at the university for a gallery or theatre visit and hungry, avail yourself of some refreshments at the refectory. The complex consists of the Arlott Bar, Terrace Restaurant, Lattes Café Bar and Hartley Brasserie.

🔺 *Sculpture in the garden of the John Hansard Gallery*

The levels of formality and the menu change slightly depending on which place you pick, but the whole venue has a lively, canteen atmosphere, and it can be enjoyable to listen in on the heated lunchtime political debates of earnest students. Newspapers are provided, and there are other student accoutrements such as a pool table in the Arlott Bar. ⓐ University campus ⓒ 09.00–18.00 Mon–Thur, 09.00–21.00 Fri, closed Sat & Sun, shorter hours outside term time

Studio Café Bar £–££ ㉘ Perfectly in harmony with its thespian–academic location, the Studio Café Bar is adorned with arty prints, including photos of past productions, drapes and generally purple décor. Baguettes, ciabattas, jackets, salads and soup complement a changing evening menu. ⓐ Nuffield Theatre ⓣ 023 8067 1771 ⓒ 10.30–14.30, 18.00–23.00 Mon–Fri, 18.00–23.00 Sat; food served 12.00–14.30 & 18.00–19.00

AFTER DARK

ARTS VENUES
The Nuffield Theatre ㉙ The packed programme of events is every bit as diverse, unusual and thought-provoking as you would expect from a university concern – Southampton's only professional producing theatre. Some of the events are participatory, and as most productions run for one or two nights only, there's a constant stream of fresh brain fodder. ⓐ University Road ⓣ 023 8067 1771 ⓦ www.nuffieldtheatre.co.uk ⓒ Box office usually 10.00–18.00 or 19.00 Mon–Sat, reduced hours in summer, hours can vary ⓝ Bus: U1, U2, U6, 6 & 11

Turner Sims Concert Hall ㉚ Classical, jazz, folk and world music all take their place in the line-up of the 60 or so concerts that this three-decade-old university venue hosts in a year. Notable performers have included Hayley Westenra, Courtney Pine and Jamie Cullum. Esteemed personages also give the occasional talk. A plus point, particularly in warm weather, is the garden setting. ⓐ Next to John Hansard Gallery, University of Southampton Highfield Campus ⓣ 023 8059 5151 ⓦ www.southampton.ac.uk/turner_sims ◷ Box office 10.00–17.00 Mon–Fri, closed Sat & Sun Bus: U1, U2, U6, 6 & 11

PUBS

The Cowherds Public House ££ ㉛ Well-managed rustic-style pub (think piles of logs and low beamed ceilings) that is something of an institution, having been around since the 1760s. The British pub grub is ideal for filling a hole when you've been tramping around the common. ⓐ Southampton Common, just off The Avenue ⓣ 023 8055 8405 ⓦ www.vintageinns.co.uk ◷ Pub 11.00–23.00 daily; food 12.00–22.00 Mon–Sat, 12.00–21.30 Sun

A quaint thatched cottage in The New Forest

OUT OF TOWN
trips

Isle of Wight

England's largest island, a county in its own right, lies 5–8 km (3–5 miles) off the coast of Hampshire, separated by the Solent. Holidaymakers have been tripping over to the Isle of Wight since Victorian times, attracted by the sort of bucolic scenery that is usually found only on commemorative biscuit tins. While in the past, some derided the island's rural charms as somewhat twee and unexciting – somewhere that you might have gone on a school journey back in the day – latterly the place has undergone something of a reinvention: a subtle demographic shift has occurred, and younger tourists are now coming in, drawn by cultural events and fashion-forward hotels. But whatever camp you fall into, the Isle of Wight's charms are undeniable, and it's easy to see what convinced Queen Victoria herself and Alfred Lord Tennyson to shift across the Solent permanently and Winston Churchill and Karl Marx to visit (though not together!). The official site of Isle of Wight Tourism is Ⓦ www.islandbreaks.co.uk

To get to the island you are compelled to make what is said to be the world's most expensive ferry journey per mile. Boats, operated by **Red Funnel** (Ⓦ www.redfunnel.co.uk), leave from Town Quay; which terminal depends on whether you want the fast service or the vehicle ferry. Either way, you'll be there in under an hour. Though of course it's more convenient to take your own car, the Isle of Wight is readily navigable on public transport. The bus network is run by **Southern Vectis** (Ⓦ www.islandbuses.info) and there are trains on the island operated by **South West Trains** (Ⓦ www.southwesttrains.co.uk), as well as a steam railway (ⓦ www.iwsteamrailway.co.uk). An alternative to public transport is cycling; bikes can be rented once you arrive. How far you want to go will obviously depend on the time you have. The compact size of the island allows you to see a fair bit in one day; if your schedule is more relaxed, overnighting clears the way for a fuller, more leisurely exploration, perhaps with some walking, cycling or watersports thrown in.

SIGHTS & ATTRACTIONS

Alum Bay

A visit to Alum Bay, to the far west of the island, affords the visitor a glimpse of one of the Isle of Wight's iconic images – the multi-

⬥ *East Cowes*

coloured sand cliffs that result from the bay's unique geological make up (something to do with Eocene beds, Cretaceous chalk formation and Alpine orogeny). An open-top bus makes the journey here in summer, and the view can be admired from the chairlift that travels up and down the cliffs. The bay is also on the tourist trail on account of its proximity to The Needles, the row of three extraordinary chalk stacks that protrude from the sea alongside a lighthouse. Take a boat trip to admire these phenomena from close range (Ⓦ www.needlespleasurecruises.co.uk).

Cowes

It's all about the boats at the Isle of Wight's northernmost point. Nautical goings-on are an indelible part of the town's history, and one that is still celebrated today in events such as **Cowes Week** (Ⓦ www.cowesweek.co.uk) in August, when posh people descend on the place and mingle with the more serious yachting fraternity. The Cowes Floating Bridge, a chain ferry, links the town with East Cowes, the other side of the estuary. Here you can pop along to **Osborne House**, Queen Victoria's old pad, and marvel at the imperial bling on show. Ⓦ www.english-heritage.org.uk

Pick up a free copy of *Island Visitor* magazine from the Town Quay ferry terminal to help you plan every aspect of your expedition, from where to stay, shop and eat to what to see and do. The *Official Summer Pocket Guide* and *Winter Pocket Guide* are available on the ferries and are also useful.

🕐 10.00–17.00 daily (Apr–Sept), 10.00–16.00 daily (Oct),
10.00–16.00 Wed–Sun and bank holidays (Nov–Mar)
ℹ Admission charge

Newport

The Isle of Wight's county town, just north of the centre of the
island, is generally visited for **Carisbrooke Castle**, the 12th-century
motte-and-bailey stronghold in which Charles I was imprisoned
in the run-up to his trial and execution for high treason. A
museum at the site illuminates his sorry plight and the stories
of other royal residents. ⓦ www.english-heritage.org.uk
🕐 10.00–17.00 daily (Apr–Sept), 10.00–16.00 daily (Oct–Mar)
ℹ Admission charge

Shanklin

On the east coast, Shanklin encapsulates the English village as
it ought to look: thatched roofs atop rustic cottages flanking
meandering country lanes. The town's two beaches and its
esplanade are the big hits with tourists, and every appurtenance
the holidaymaker could dream of is likely to be provided here by
one of the many businesses that have sprung up to cater for the
streams of visitors.

TAKING A BREAK

The Vineleaf Coffee Shop ££ England doesn't have many coffee
shops where you can enjoy a glass of wine from the vineyard
you're in. Besides the award-winning vino, there's a range of light
bites, snacks, cream teas, cakes and hot drinks. ⓐ Smallbrook Lane,

Ryde ☎ 01983 811084 🌐 www.rosemaryvineyard.co.uk 🕐 10.00–17.00 Mon–Sat, 11.00–16.00 Sun (Apr–Sept); 10.00–16.00 Mon–Sat, 11.00–16.00 Sun (Oct–Mar) closed Sun in Feb & Mar

Warren Farm Tea Rooms ££ This working farm's cream teas are much garlanded, having been pronounced one of Britain's best by both the *Guardian* and the BBC. Made with local produce in the farm's Aga, homemade cakes and scones are accompanied by light lunches and fabulous views. 📍 Alum Bay ☎ 01983 753200 🌐 www.farmhousecreamteas.co.uk 🕐 12.00–17.30 Sat, Sun & holidays (Easter–May & Oct); 12.00–17.30 Sat–Thur, closed Fri (June–Sept); closed Nov–Easter 🚌 Bus: 7

RESTAURANTS

Murrays ££ Cowes's oldest seafood restaurant ain't broke so nobody's trying to fix it. The fare includes piscatorial standards such as fish soup, moules marinière and crab Marie Rose. Go for the set menu for maximum value. 📍 106 High Street ☎ 01983 296233 🌐 www.murrays.uk.com 🕐 12.00–14.30, 19.00–21.30 Mon–Sat, 12.30–14.30, 19.00–21.30 Sun

The Cameron restaurant £££ The four-course table d'hôte menu draws on local seasonal ingredients, and there's a changing à la carte menu too. The elegance of the dining room with its bay views might suggest that a meal here would divest you of a significant sum, but both menus in fact provide excellent value. 📍 Bourne Hall Hotel, 11 Luccombe Road, Shanklin ☎ 01983 862820 🌐 www.bournehallhotel.co.uk

The New Forest

England cannot have many places that engender such a sense of contentment as the New Forest on a sunny day. Now Britain's smallest national park, the forest (something of a misnomer: much of the wooded area of yore has given way to open, treeless land) is 571 sq km (220 sq miles) of British beauty – heather, gorse, grass, heath and practically every other green thing that grows. There are several specific attractions – not least the iconic New Forest Pony – but the park's main joy lies in simply admiring its superb panoramas, so exquisite that they could turn anyone into a poet. The website of the New Forest National Park Authority is ⓦ www.newforestnpa.gov.uk

From Southampton you can take either a bus (Ⓝ 8, 9, 10, 11, 12, 56, 56A, X5, X7, X71, N9) or a train into the park; it's sensible to

◗ *The native ponies graze freely in the New Forest*

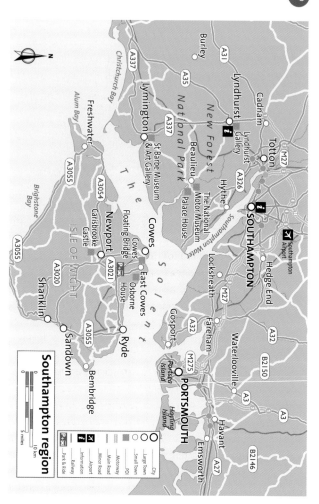

Southampton region

consult timetables before setting off as some of the services are hourly. Understandably, the authority would rather visitors eschewed their cars, but nothing is actively done to discourage drivers and you will find reasonably priced spots to park in the towns. Numerous cycle hire outlets advertise themselves in Lyndhurst's information centre.

SIGHTS & ATTRACTIONS

Beaulieu

Beautiful Beaulieu (in the time-honoured, outsider-frustrating English village way, it's actually pronounced Bew-ley), in the southeast of the national park, serves as a physical embodiment of the British class system: it's the seat of the Montagu family, old-school landed gentry. Though your mind may briefly linger on how pleasant it would be to obtain such an appealing country pile by birthright, ownership issues will not dent your enjoyment of the estate, parts of which are open to the public (though you may baulk at the hefty admission fee!). The **National Motor Museum** (perhaps a rather incongruous facility for a national park – the current m'lud is something of a car enthusiast) is the main attraction. In the same complex is **Palace House**, the Montagu digs, which has the air of the sort of mansion in which an aristocratically dysfunctional family in an Agatha Christie novel might set about bumping each other off. ⓐ 12 km (7½ miles) southeast of Lyndhurst ⓦ www.beaulieu. co.uk 🕙 10.00–17.00 daily (Oct–May); 10.00–18.00 (June–Sept) ⓘ Admission charge

Lyndhurst

Pretty Lyndhurst is a useful starting point for exploration of the New Forest and is home to the **New Forest Visitor Centre** (ⓐ Off High Street in main car park ⓣ 023 8028 2269 ⓦ www.thenewforest.co.uk ⓛ 10.00–17.00 daily). As well as furnishing interested parties with a free park newspaper, *New Forest Focus*, which contains a helpful map and events listings, and suggesting itineraries, they can book accommodation and also stock an assortment of leaflets. In the same building is a small gallery hosting temporary exhibits which change every six weeks.

There's also a museum here (ⓘ admission charge) charting the story of the New Forest, its native pony and commoners (they're not being snobby – the word means smallholders and farmers), along with fascinating panels on New Forest gypsies as well as snake catching and crime – smuggling and poaching. Interactivity weaves its way throughout and younger visitors will love the dressing up box. Outside the centre a wall of notices advertises local events and services, including jazz, craft fairs, galleries, walks and flea markets.

While you're in Lyndhurst, you might like to wander along the High Street (going up the hill) to the imposing Victorian **Church of St Michael & All Angels** (ⓣ 023 8028 2154 ⓦ www. newforestparishes.com). Inside, the high ceiling, stained glass windows and mural combine to great effect, and you'll find plenty of information on the history. The town is chock full of tea rooms so it's also a handy spot for lunch. ⓐ 13 km (8 miles) southwest of Southampton

Lymington

Lying at the south of the national park, ferries go from Lymington across the Solent to the Isle of Wight, making it easy to combine the two excursion destinations covered in this guide. With three marinas, Lymington is also popular with yachties. Visitors can amble along cobbled streets, admiring the Georgian architecture, or visit the **St Barbe Museum & Art Gallery**. ⓐ New Street ① 01590 676969 ⓦ www.stbarbe-museum.org.uk ① 10.00–16.00 Mon–Sat, closed Sun, last entry 15.30 ① Admission charge

RETAIL THERAPY

Lyndhurst Gallery A changing exhibition of work by contemporary British artists. ⓐ 68 High Street ① 023 8028 3243 ⓦ www.lyndhurstgallery.co.uk ① 10.00–17.00 Wed–Mon, closed Tues

Lyndhurst Antiques and Collectables Two floors brimming with the eponymous items. ⓐ 19/21 High Street ① 023 8028 4000 ⓦ www.lyndhurstantiques.com ① 10.00–17.00 daily (summer); 10.00–16.00 Mon–Fri, 10.00–17.00 Sat & Sun (winter)

TAKING A BREAK

CAFÉS
The Lyndhurst Tea House ££ Homely, bright and cheerful, this place bustles with happy patrons tucking into sandwiches, paninis, pasta, salad and old favourites like rarebit.

🄰 26 High Street 🄣 023 8028 2656 🄧 09.00–16.00 Mon–Fri, 09.00–16.30 Sat, 10.00–16.30 Sun

Mad Hatter Tea Rooms ££ This traditional establishment looks like it has changed little over the last few decades, and is much the nicer for it. Quaint window displays in front of net curtains, service with a smile and an inviting roof terrace add to the ambience. 🄰 10 High Street 🄣 023 8028 2341 🄧 09.30–16.00 Mon–Fri, 09.30–17.00 Sat & Sun

RESTAURANTS & PUBS

The White Hart ££ Rest yourself a while by the roaring log fire and enjoy old-school hospitality at this 200-year-old inn, which serves main meals and snacks throughout the day. 🄰 17 Milford Road, Lymington 🄣 01590 673495 🄦 www.pubsnewforest.co.uk

Master Builder's £££ The adventurous menu, on which lobster and duck both feature, fashioned into tempting posh nosh, is entirely in keeping with this swanky country pile.
🄰 Buckler's Hard, Beaulieu Estate 🄣 0844 815 3399
🄦 www.themasterbuilders.co.uk

This way to walk the old city walls

WALK THE SOUTHAMPTON WALLS

↔

PRACTICAL
information

Directory

GETTING THERE
By air
Southampton Airport is served primarily by two airlines: Flybe (Ⓦ www.flybe.com), with flights from 17 UK towns and cities and more than 30 European cities; and Eastern Airways (Ⓦ www.easternairways.com), which flies from Aberdeen, Durham Tees Valley, Leeds Bradford, Liverpool and Stavanger.

Many people are aware that air travel emits CO_2, which contributes to climate change. You may be interested in the possibility of lessening the environmental impact of your flight through the charity **Climate Care** (Ⓦ www.jpmorgan climatecare.com) which offsets your CO_2 by funding environmental projects around the world.

By car
Driving can be the most economical way of reaching Southampton if you're travelling in a group. From London, the city is about 120 km (75 miles) away. Take the M3, and leave at junction 14 for the A33, which takes you all the way into town. The AA website route planner (Ⓦ www.theaa.com) can give you a detailed breakdown of the journey and a map.

By coach
In the UK, coaches tend to take longer than trains but they are generally cheaper. National Express coaches (Ⓦ www.nationalexpress.com) serve Southampton from various UK cities, although if you're coming from the north

you will probably have to change in London, from where there are around a dozen daily services. The official journey time is slightly over two hours, but in practice the buses often seem to arrive ahead of schedule. If you can book in advance and are flexible over times there are some good-value fares on offer.

By rail

Train is often the quickest way of reaching Southampton. (Ⓦ www.nationalrail.co.uk). Journey times from London Waterloo vary between 1¼ and 1½ hours, and there are about four services an hour.

GETTING AROUND

Buses

Blue Star Ⓦ www.bluestarbus.co.uk
First Group Ⓦ www.firstgroup.com
Stagecoach Ⓦ www.stagecoachbus.com
Uni-link Ⓦ www.unilinkbus.co.uk
Wilts & Dorset Ⓦ www.wdbus.co.uk

Car hire

Avis Ⓦ www.avis.co.uk
Budget Ⓦ www.budget.co.uk
Europcar Ⓦ www.europcar.co.uk
Hertz Ⓦ www.hertz.co.uk
National Ⓦ www.nationalcar.co.uk
Sixt Ⓦ www.sixt.co.uk
Thrifty Ⓦ www.thrifty.co.uk

HEALTH, SAFETY & CRIME

Southampton is no more dangerous than the average British city, but the usual travel advice applies: keep your valuables safe, don't wander into deserted areas (including the common) alone after dark and avoid the vicinity of pubs and clubs at 'chucking out time' if you prefer not to witness raucous scenes. If you take to the water then take the appropriate safety precautions.

Southampton Police Station ⓐ Civic Centre, Havelock Road ⓣ 999 or 112 for emergencies; 101 for non-emergencies; 0845 045 4545 for Hampshire Police HQ in Winchester ⓦ www.hampshire.police.uk ⓒ 24 hours

Southampton General Hospital ⓐ Tremona Road ⓣ 023 8079 6220 (Accident & Emergency) ⓦ www.suht.nhs.uk

For non-urgent medical help, the **NHS Direct** line is ⓣ 0845 46 47, or you can go online at ⓦ www.nhsdirect.nhs.uk

OPENING HOURS

Some of Southampton's tourist attractions seem to operate for fewer hours in winter than is the norm for a British city, and if you turn up at a museum or gallery at 15.45 it's not unusual for the place to be closing for the day. In general, attractions open from 10.00 (give or take an hour) to somewhere between 16.00 and 18.00, depending on the season, and tend to close on Monday. Shopping hours are around 09.00 or 09.30 to 17.00 or 18.00 for six days. Trading law limits Sunday opening to six hours.

CHILDREN

While older kids may enjoy some of the museums, especially those big on interactivity, like the **City Art Gallery** (see page 64),

or the humungous planes at **Solent Sky Aviation Museum** (see pages 52–3), younger children will love the outdoor amusements of the New Forest or Isle of Wight. Several child-friendly attractions orbit Southampton, including **Marwell Zoo** (Ⓦ www.marwell.org.uk), **Paulton's Family Theme Park** (Ⓦ www.paultonspark.co.uk), **Manor Farm** (Ⓦ www3.hants.gov.uk), **Long Down Dairy Farm** (Ⓦ www.longdownfarm.co.uk) and **Romsey Rapids** (Ⓦ www.the-rapids.co.uk). Within town, **Southampton Common** (see pages 71–3) and the **Hawthorns Urban Wildlife Centre** (see pages 70–71) will keep younger holidaymakers well entertained.

TRAVELLERS WITH DISABILITIES

While the more modern facilities and all university venues are wheelchair accessible, and moves are being made to open up more of the city to disabled visitors (such as the lift being installed at Tudor House Museum), some of the attractions will be partially off limits for logistical reasons. The council website has a page with general advice, and attraction-specific information such as number of stairs. Much of the city centre is flat and pedestrianised.

FURTHER INFORMATION

The city's **Tourist Information Centre** stocks a wealth of leaflets, free maps of town and can book accommodation. *Listed* magazine has a Southampton edition and an online version (Ⓦ www.listedmagazine.com).

Tourist Information Centre ⓐ 9 Civic Centre Road ⓣ 023 8083 3333 Ⓦ www.visit-southampton.co.uk ⓛ 09.30–17.00 Mon–Sat, 10.00–15.30 Sun & bank holidays

ACKNOWLEDGEMENTS
The photographs in this book were taken by Grant Rooney for Thomas Cook Publishing, to whom the copyright belongs.

Project editor: Rosalind Munro
Copy editor: Kate Taylor
Proofreaders: Ceinwen Sinclair & Michele Greenbank
Layout: Donna Pedley
Indexer: Marie Lorimer

AUTHOR BIOGRAPHY
Debbie Stowe is a freelance journalist, travel writer and author. She has written around 20 non-fiction and travel books, specialising in UK destinations, among others. Her writing also covers the natural world, film, human rights, cultural and social issues.

Send your thoughts to
books@thomascook.com

- Found a great bar, club, shop or must-see sight that we don't feature?
- Like to tip us off about any information that needs a little updating?
- Want to tell us what you love about this handy little guidebook and more importantly how we can make it even handier?

Then here's your chance to tell all! Send us ideas, discoveries and recommendations today and then look out for your valuable input in the next edition of this title.

Email the above address (stating the title) or write to:
pocket guides Series Editor, Thomas Cook Publishing, PO Box 227, Coningsby Road, Peterborough PE3 8SB, UK.